Bringing Nature Home

FLORAL ARRANGEMENTS INSPIRED BY NATURE

Text & photography by Ngoc Minh Ngo

arrangements by
NICOLETTE OWEN

prop styling by
AMY WILSON

foreword by
DEBORAH NEEDLEMAN

RIZZOLI
NEW YORK

New York Paris London Milan

Dedicated to the memory of my father, who taught me the meaning of home and shared my love of flowers

Contents

Foreword

A ROOM IS NEVER AT ITS BEST without flowers. Flowers show that a home is cared for and truly lived in. While furniture can remain the same for years, flowers speak to the present moment. And yet they are a talisman, a reminder of the world beyond our doors, of growth and change, and the passage of time. They are fleeting pleasures.

Ngoc's book is a sonnet to the seasons. It rejoices in the beauties particular to each, and to the immense joy to be had from paying witness to those changes, and of bringing its fruits into the home. That is the message of this book, made abundantly clear through Ngoc's text and the effect of her poetic photographs. But underlying that, her pictures also reveal her expansive appreciation for the variety of ways flowers have been used in different cultures and times in history.

There is an appreciation of the Japanese aesthetic in these pages—the idea that a single bloom can evoke an entire meadow, or one flowering branch the woods. A traditional Japanese bouquet is not a mixed one full of flowers, but a more economical, thoughtful arrangement of a single stem or careful balance of just a few. One peony blossom in a bottle, or just a few flowering branches in a vase, is enough.

But there is also something very French to this book and to Ngoc's sensibility. Since the nineteenth century, Paris has had open markets and flower carts, which have created a culture in which flowers are not special-occasion things, but rather an everyday part of a good life. Many of the bouquets call to mind something a *Parisienne* might happen to pick up at the market on her walk home, like a bunch of daffodils in spring or dahlias in late summer.

And yet there are also images of loose, spontaneous clusters of flowers that look like wild gardens captured in a vase. These reference the British love for wandering into the field, or into the garden, and gathering together whatever one happens to find blooming. It is this tradition that brings us those wonderfully charming bunches of wildflowers mixed with garden roses and vines that practically spill over the edges of an old jam jar or pitcher.

But here too, there is a sensibility that is uniquely American. This book inspires a Thoreau-ean sense of the transcendence of nature—a sense that the great outdoors is our Walden, and that even large maple branches or a bunch of woodland daisies can a beautiful, awe-inspiring bouquet make.

The flower arrangements in this book are the handiwork of Nicolette Owen. She herself embraces all these traditions—even operating a delightfully retro flower stall in Brooklyn from time to time—but she seems the direct heir to the greatest of all florists, the Englishwoman Constance Spry. For Spry no leaf or weed or vegetable pod was out of the question if it could contribute to an arrangement. In the 1930s, she made hosta leaves and seed heads and tufts of grasses and other things (that were, until then, *flora non grata*) incredibly chic. Spry's artistry was beloved by the aristocracy, yet she often used the humblest of materials and made us look again more closely at their charms. Nicolette, like Spry, favors groupings in which some tree foliage might mix it up with both wild and cultivated flowers. Nicolette often draws upon the typically unnoticed aspects of a flower: matching the slight variation in its petal color or the shimmering silver of its berries to other elements that somewhere on them share that hue. Through Nicolette's subtle blends of color, one sees flowers anew: an anemone as if one never saw one before—more its black center than its pink petal; a hydrangea, more its underlying green than its white flowers. And from her combinations comes a new aesthetic, not of monochrome arrangements or a cacophony of colors, but a gentle hymn.

This book calls upon us to look, to appreciate, and whenever possible, to collect a bit of the outdoors to bring inside. Of course flowers are for every day, to be picked up after work with the bread and milk—and with the proliferation of farmers' markets everywhere that is now easy for us to do. Why do we too often save flowers for special occasions like a party or a thank you? While the photographs here are rich, what they show is everyday life: real rooms with real flowers, not interior-decorated homes with professional-looking displays. The quotidian nature of these images, and the moments they evoke, reveal that somehow the everyday is more special than any special occasion. **DEBORAH NEEDLEMAN**

Introduction

WE LOVE FLOWERS for their sensual quality and the emotions they elicit. With their infinitely varying forms, colors, and scents, flowers have always captured our imagination, recalling happy moments and inspiring great works of art. The author Gabriel García Márquez had a yellow rose on his desk every day for eighteen months while writing his masterpiece of magical realism *One Hundred Years of Solitude*. In his book *The Artist in His Studio*, Alexander Liberman described in painstaking detail the modest home in which Alberto Giacometti lived and worked for most of his life. It was a shabby place with cracked paint, a few simple pieces of furniture, a mattress on the floor, a drying line hanging in a corner, an old radio, a plate burner, innumerable newspapers, and a few volumes of poetry. Amid all this stood a modest pitcher of flowers, a simple bouquet that added a "spark of emotional relief" without which the "room would seem unbearable." Such is the power of a few gathered flowers in a room.

People have been arranging flowers in one form or another since the beginning of civilization. Formal bouquets decorate banquet tables on murals found in Egyptian tombs that date as far back as the fourteenth century BC. In ancient China, the art of flower arrangement was greatly prized during the Han Dynasty. Chinese Buddhist monks in the late fifth century made large symmetrical arrangements of brightly colored flowers in bronze vases to decorate the altars, a practice that was later adapted and expanded upon in Japan, where the highly refined art form of *Ikebana* was born.

Europeans during the Dark Ages led restricted and spartan lives, and the art of floral decoration was forgotten. Flowers were cultivated for their usefulness in medicine rather than their beauty. Gothic illuminated manuscripts show the occasional simple bouquets placed in utilitarian containers. It was not until the early Renaissance that flowers regained their place in home decoration. In a noble house, elaborate flower arrangements could be used to brighten a room or freshen the air. Many paintings from the period showed vases of flowers adorning tables, mantels, windowsills, and alcoves in interior scenes. In Hans Holbein The Younger's *Study for the Family Portrait of Sir Thomas More*, dated 1527, there are three different floral arrangements placed around the room.

The age of trade and exploration brought exotic plants from the East to Europe, and many of the new flowers became luxury commodities. Seventeenth-century Dutch and Flemish flower paintings have left us with exquisite depictions of sumptuous bouquets. Featuring the most desirable blooms of the time—tulips, roses, carnations, and hyacinths, to name a few—these magnificent paintings were not inspired by actual bouquets since they incorporate flowers from different seasons. More an expression of desire than a reflection of reality, such compositions nonetheless have left a lasting influence on the art of flower arrangement.

The Victorian age in England ushered in a new era in floral decoration. Queen Victoria herself was passionate about having cut flowers in every room. There was a proliferation of magazines and books dispensing advice on the subject of floral decoration. No proper young lady's education was complete without lessons in the art of arranging flowers. The wealthy had large gardens set aside to provide cut flowers for their estates. Gardeners dispatched flowers from the country onto the night train to arrive in the morning for the decoration of town houses. Extensive greenhouse cultivation also made it possible to have fresh flowers any time of the year. Today cut flowers adorn houses large and small all over the world.

Throughout history flowers have commanded admiration and symbolized complex emotions for people of all cultures. The ephemeral nature of flowers whose blooms come fleetingly once a year to claim our admiration only adds to their enchantment. Flowers and plants are dulcet emblems of the natural world—messengers from the landscape to herald the seasons. They are points of light that sustain us with their beauty. Through the ages, people have brought flowers and foliage into their homes for different reasons: to cheer up a dark corner, to fill a room with fragrance, or simply to enjoy up close the complex architecture of a flower or the intricately varying hues on the autumn leaves. In today's increasingly hectic and stressful world, the home is far more significant than just a place of shelter. It is "a still point of a turning world," to borrow an exquisite phrase from T. S. Eliot's meditation on the nature of time. We want our homes to be expressions of ourselves, and different flowers speak to our psychic need for beauty. The simple act of cutting flowers to bring into one's home comes naturally to anyone who has ever gathered a bouquet of dandelions as a child. Gardeners instinctively bring indoors cut flowers and foliage as a way of charting the rhythm of the seasons, mapping out the months of the year with every bloom and leaf: a spray of lilacs in April, a single stem of peony for the month of June, rose hips in September, and the brilliant maple leaves in October. Like the ancient Chinese who could contemplate the whole cosmos embodied in a few flowers or a branch, gardeners can appreciate the entire life cycle of a single flower, from its growing bud to its fading form, and see the important lessons that flowers can teach us about the passage of time.

Traditional Japanese homes since the fourteenth century have a specially built niche, called *tokonoma*, where a vase of flowers and calligraphic scrolls are displayed for contemplation. Bring a flower or plant indoors to look at it individually and you will learn to appreciate its unique brand of beauty—for instance, the way the petals of the carnation are finely ruffled at the edge brings to mind layers of crinkled silk on the skirt of a ball gown. Look closely at the petals of an unfolding garden rose and you will understand what Rainer Maria Rilke meant when he wrote, "I see you, rose, half-open book filled with so many pages of that detailed happiness we will never read." By bringing tiny bits of nature into our home, we make the vital connection to the ever-changing natural world outside. Each season that unfurls itself on the landscape offers its own treasures. The lacy patterns of naked branches against a winter sky can be as enchanting as the sight of unassuming Queen Anne's lace waving in the wind by the roadside in the summer.

Flowers have been thought at times to be a useless extravagance. At the end of the Roman Empire, war and religious strife kept all cultivation of plants strictly to the necessity of food and medicine. In China, during the Cultural Revolution, Mao viewed floral decoration as a frivolous capitalist luxury, which led people to uproot flowers and smash flowerpots. But as Alexander Liberman attested so movingly in his description of Giacometti's home, a few gathered flowers can breathe life into the most abject place. So make room in your home for some flowers. Just a single branch of flowering quince to watch its buds unfold. Or a handful of tiny grape hyacinths to celebrate the spring. According to a saying attributed to the prophet Mohammed, "Bread feeds the body, indeed, but flowers feed also the soul."

Spring

Summer
Autumn
Winter

"We tell you
of a blossoming
and buds
in every tree."

ANONYMOUS, "Old May Song"

The Japanese custom of viewing cherry blossoms, *hanami*, dates back for centuries. Annual flower-viewing parties were held at the Imperial Court to celebrate the spectacular and ephemeral beauty of cherry blossoms. The custom eventually spread to the Samurai class and to the common people. By the seventeenth century, farmers developed their own *hanami* custom by climbing nearby mountains to have lunch under the flowering cherry trees. Have your own *hanami* with an exuberant arrangement of cherry tree branches at home. What better way to celebrate spring than to wake up under a cloud of cherry blossoms?

The poppy anemones, first cultivated in the sixteenth century, are models of versatility. Throw a bunch of bright purple poppy anemones in a simple glass jar to add a cheerful note to a child's room, or put a few elegant stems in sleek white ceramic bottles to admire their subtle loveliness from every angle.

Spring's greatest wonders are flowering branches and bulbs. Blooming alongside cherry blossoms, crab apple flowers range in colors from pearly white to delicate pink to deep red. Choose a beautifully shaped large vase to showcase the floaty blossoms on the branches. OPPOSITE Grape hyacinths are tiny blue marvels that carpet the woodlands in mid-spring. Fill a glass full of these beauties to enjoy their clusters of tiny, urn-shaped flowers in finely drawn hues of blue at home. Though they bloom in April, their spicy-grape fragrance has been described as "the perfume of clove and sun-warmed Concord grapes of late September."

Flowering dogwoods are among the most enchanting trees in the spring garden, when their bare twigs are smothered in dazzling pink and white blossoms. Mixed with dark mauve hellebores and matching pink ranunculus, dogwood blossoms anchor this bright spring bouquet. Green corydalis and dark purple coral bell foliage add contrasting textures.

Peony *Paeonia*

PAEONIA is named after Paeon, the Greek gods' personal physician, said by Homer in *The Iliad* to have healed both Ares, the god of war wounded in battle with the mortal Diomedes, and Hades, the god of the underworld injured by Herakles's arrow.

Since ancient times the tree peony (*Paeonia suffruticosa*) has been a favorite flower in China, where it is the symbol of wealth, fortune, luck, prosperity, and happiness. The Chinese name for peony is "sho yu," meaning most beautiful, and no other flower can rival its extravagant beauty. Eighteenth-century travelers to China were enchanted by this ancient flower, which they described as resembling a gigantic rose without thorns. Since its introduction to Europe in 1787, the voluptuous peony has enthralled Western florists and held a special place in the garden. Devoted French, English, and American horticulturalists in the last two centuries have created a vast array of hybrids with a dizzying variety of forms and colors, from deep crimson to pale pink, pristine white, and delicate yellow.

The seductive beauty of peonies has also held artists spellbound for thousands of years. Peonies are one of the main motifs on Chinese porcelain and screen paintings. Poems and stories about the peony abound in Chinese and Japanese literature. In the West, Henri Fantin-Latour and Edouard Manet painted some of the most exquisite peonies on canvas.

One of the most beautiful collections of tree peonies can be found at the Brooklyn Botanic Garden. After the events of September 11, 2001, the people of the Japanese town Yatsuka-Cho in Shimane Prefecture, renowned for the cultivation of rare tree peonies, sent to the Brooklyn Botanic Garden and Rockefeller State Park Preserve more than one thousand tree peonies as a gesture of solidarity, hoping that they could bring comfort and healing to New York. Unfortunately, the plants perished as they sat in hot, dry containers on a dock in Long Beach, California, while a strike by the longshoremen's union shut down the West Coast ports. Yatsuka-Cho sent a new shipment, which included three hundred specimens for the Brooklyn Botanic Garden that arrived in December. Despite being planted during a blizzard in half-frozen soil, these plants managed to survive. Every year in early May, they burst into bloom, with flowers the size of dinner plates that manage to be both overblown and elegant at the same time, bringing much joy and happiness to the garden's visitors.

Peonies are unabashedly voluptuous even as they age. These slightly-on-the-wane coral peonies fade into a beguiling pale yellow, their blooms just as ravishing as the delicate blush pink peonies that are on the cusp of opening (opposite).

The color range of peonies includes countless beautiful shades, some just a slight shift in the spectrum from one another. Fill a vase with a mix of subtly different hues of the same color, or enjoy a striking bouquet of peonies all in the same intense red (opposite).

Bleeding heart is a spring ephemeral plant that starts blooming in April and becomes dormant when the heat of the summer sets in. The heart-shaped blooms dangling on arching stems make charming cut flowers, and the finely divided foliage is a thing of beauty on its own.

There is nothing more cheerful than the sight of daffodils in bloom at the end of a long winter. In his famous poem in honor of the flower, William Wordsworth described coming upon a field of ten thousand daffodils "tossing their heads in sprightly dance," a memory that forever filled his heart with pleasure. Gather a couple of different varieties of daffodils—there are more than 25,000 registered cultivars—for the breakfast table, or mix them with pansies, Solomon's seal, mint, and bleeding heart foliage to make a sweet and cheery bouquet.

Another prized flower of the spring garden is azalea, whose profuse blooms come in vibrant colors. Arrange branches of pink azalea in a pretty blue ceramic vase to emphasize their graceful charm. OPPOSITE This delightful bouquet combines some of the best of spring blooms in the garden. Dainty crab apple blossoms, pendulous bleeding hearts, wispy fritillaries, and elegant tulips are anchored by curly geranium leaves in a wonderful play of colors, shapes, and textures.

Lilac season begins in April and continues through May, filling the landscape with its ineffable perfume that stirs up memories and fills us with nostalgia. T. S. Eliot wrote, "April is the cruellest month, breeding lilacs out of the dead land, mixing memory and desire," while Longfellow once declared, "I shall not be likely to go to town while the lilacs bloom." Few can resist the beauty of lilacs, which make extravagant spring bouquets. Here, lilacs are complemented with other spring blooms: ravishing fringed tulips, smoky hellebores, elegant bearded irises, and wispy stems of spirea.

Mountain laurels inhabit rocky slopes and mountainous forests all along the East Coast of North America. In May and June these evergreen shrubs erupt in clusters of cup-shaped pink and white flowers along the roadsides. A few branches in a simple large glass jar make a spectacular arrangement in any home. OPPOSITE A spring garden bouquet of tulips, hyacinths, and pink jasmine, mixed with corydalis and five-leaf akebia, has the elegance of a Dutch flower painting and the palette of a vibrant Impressionist canvas.

Fritillary *Fritillaria meleagris*

THE UNUSUAL *Fritillaria meleagris* is a native plant of damp meadows throughout northwestern Europe, where it usually grows in large colonies. Its many common names—Checkered Lily, Chess Flower, and fritillary (from the Latin *frittilus*, meaning dice box)—refer to its unique checkered pattern. It is also known as the Snake's Head Lily because the shape of its unopened bud resembles the striking pose of a cobra. The beauty of the fritillary comes from not only its checker pattern (unique among all flowers) but also its delicate architecture. The bell-shaped fritillary flower, in deep purple or white, dangles daintily at the end of an arching stem, surrounded by curlicue foliage.

The fritillary appeared in medieval tapestries but only entered the garden in the sixteenth century. It was first brought to England from France in 1572 by a druggist named Noel Caperon. Known as Caperon's Narcissus, the fritillary became a regular feature in the Elizabethan garden, though it was later discovered that *Fritillaria meleagris* had always grown in the wild in England. It remains popular in both English and French cultivated gardens but the flower has become endangered from habitat loss and is now rarely found in the wild.

In England, fritillary meadows—a common sight before World War II—have all but disappeared in recent years. Efforts to protect the fritillary have led to a slow comeback in the south. Today one of the best fritillary meadows is at Magdalen College in Oxford, where *Fritillaria meleagris* has been known to flourish since 1785. Bordered by the River Cherwell, the meadow is often flooded in wet winters, providing the perfect habitat for these moisture-loving flowers. Every spring, they put on a charming show, filling the ten-acre meadow with their nodding purple blooms for two to three weeks.

Unlike the blockbuster appeal of tulips, the downward-facing fritillary's beauty only reveals itself to those who take the trouble to look at it closely. Its unique checker pattern has fascinated generations of botanists, painters, and poets. In his poem "Panthea," Oscar Wilde wrote:

> "On sunless days in winter, we shall know
> By whom the silver gossamer is spun,
> Who paints the diapered fritillaries,
> On what wide wings from shivering pine
> To pine the eagle flies."

For a brief spell in spring, the marvelous fritillaries peek their nodding heads out of the ground to charm us with their inimitable beauty. Enjoy their distinctive architecture in a wispy cluster or just two elegantly curving stems.

Mock orange is grown for its fragrant, white flowers that bloom abundantly in late spring through early summer. Arching stems laden with blooms make a lush arrangement that fills the room with an evocative scent, hinting at the aroma of oranges.

GUINNESS · NI
6 - : AST 2ND ST. (212)

· AT JOHN DERIAN

FLORILEGIUM IMPERIALE   PRESTEL

A simple glass decanter makes a perfect vessel for these velvety red anemones. OPPOSITE The striking crown imperial, the crowning glory in many Dutch flower paintings, has pendulous bell-shaped flowers borne in a circle and topped with a tuft of small leaves. Choose a special vase for these royal flowers to show off their uncommon form.

Few trees can rival the splendor of a flowering dogwood in bloom. Bring home an armful of flowering dogwood branches to appreciate their elegant blossoms up close. OPPOSITE Grouping different flowers in the same hue emphasizes their particular beauty. The purple ranunculus flowers here look almost prim and proper next to the arching tulips, which seem to be caught in mid-movement.

The dramatic, pink-flushed, creamy white blooms of magnolia, an ancient flower named after a French botanist, deserve close inspection. Bring indoors a few branches of budding magnolia to delight in their unfolding magnificence and exquisite scent of tropical citrus.

Mixing flowers in the same family of color is a great way to make an arrangement. Ranunculus in varying shades of reds and pinks comprise this informal bouquet. Dark red oxalis and coleus leaves add another layer of color and texture. OPPOSITE Add a couple of mauve bearded irises for an unexpected note of contrast to their yellow counterparts.

Place a couple of stems of ranunculus in a simple glass bottle by the window light to observe their paper-thin petals, each unfolding in succeeding layers like intricate origami. OPPOSITE The tiny white flowers of Thunberg spirea (deserving of its more poetic name, Breath of Spring spirea), borne on wiry dark stems, are among spring's most delicate beauties.

Spring

Summer

Autumn
Winter

"I see the wild flowers, in their summer morn
Of beauty, feeding on joy's luscious hours"

JOHN CLARE, "Summer Images"

Saturated coral-colored begonias accentuate the peachy undertone of pale pink garden roses. OPPOSITE Clematis, often called the Queen of Climbers for its regal vines with twisting tendrils, has flowers in various shapes and colors. The majestic blooms of *Clematis* 'Snow Queen' make a great contrast to the nodding bell-shaped flower of *Clematis fremontii*, both in good company with the silvery foliage of Russian olive.

The botanist Carl Linnaeus, who gave nasturtium its botanical name, *Tropaeolum*, thought its flame-orange flower resembled "a spear-pierced golden helmet with blood stains." The spicy taste of its leaves and flowers adds a peppery flavor to salads, but a trailing vine of nasturtium in bloom is a delicate feast for the eyes.

Robert Graves

D. H. Lawrence

Robert Frost

Robert Frost   D 27

Italian Verse   D 57

The New Poetry   D 63

Sick Verse   D 75

German Verse   D 36

The heavy bloom of oakleaf hydrangea 'Snowflake' is the center of attention in this menagerie of mostly white blossoms, including peonies, clematis, columbines, and pincushion flower. OPPOSITE Make the most of the marvelous plumes of smoke bush by mixing it with Japanese maple leaves tinged in the same purple-red hue for an arrangement that is as extravagant as summer itself.

This sumptuous bouquet of garden roses with its heady perfume recalls a line written by Rilke in one of his French rose poems: "Summer: to be for a few days the contemporary of roses; to breathe what's floating around their souls in bloom." OPPOSITE The green wonder of summer comes in many shades and forms. Create a lush tapestry of textures with some of the season's most interesting foliage: bright chartreuse sprirea 'Ogon', silvery artemisia, dark coral bells, fragrant oregano, and fuzzy lamb's ear.

Thick, bare stems holding plump figs make a sculptural arrangement. OPPOSITE Clematis 'Niobe' has burgundy-red flowers that turn deep magenta when backlit by the window light. A cascading vine of these beauteous blooms is one of summer's great delights.

The purple cone-flower that blooms all summer long in prairies and meadows actually comes in many other colors. A bouquet of these flowers in varying shades of pink and coppery-orange looks enchanting with purple basil. OPPOSITE Spires of pastel-colored foxgloves and white Queen Anne's lace, complemented with ferny corydalis and fuzzy plectran-thus 'Nicoletta' foliage, make up this charming garden bouquet.

Carnation *Dianthus*

THE COMMON CARNATION, known variously as pink, clove pink, and gillyflower, dyed in garish colors and readily available all year round at the deli, actually has a highly distinguished past. Writing more than two thousand years ago, the Greek botanist and philosopher Theophrastus gave its name as "Dianthus," combining the Greek words for divine ("*dios*") and flower ("*anthos*"). Through centuries, carnations were featured in works of art and literature. In Shakespeare's *The Winter's Tale*, Perdita claimed "the fairest flowers o' the season are our carnations and streaked gillyvors." It was said that the carnation first bloomed on Earth wherever the Virgin Mary shed tears along the path to Calvary. Raphael, Leonardo da Vinci, and Albrecht Durer were among the Renaissance artists whose paintings of the Virgin and Child show Mary holding out a carnation to the baby Jesus. Marriage portraits from the fifteenth and sixteenth centuries often depict one or both partners holding a carnation, a symbol of betrothal. In seventeenth-century Dutch flower paintings, the carnation was given pride of place alongside the highly prized tulips, roses, fritillaries, and other flowers.

A native of the Mediterranean region, *Dianthus caryophyllus*, the wild ancestor of the garden carnation, was originally bright pink. Its legendary spicy clove fragrance made *Dianthus* a favorite scented flower, after the rose, in the Elizabethan garden. The nearly three hundred species of *Dianthus*, with cultivars in colors of deep red, white, yellow, purple, and even green, were popularized by Oscar Wilde, who famously wore dyed green carnations on his lapel. Over a hundred years ago, the heavily scented and large double-flowered Malmaison carnation reached cult status in Edwardian England. Dating back to 1857, the Malmaison carnation originated in France, where it bloomed from a chance seedling. The new flower, with a heady scent of clove and a strong resemblance to the Bourbon rose, was named "Souvenir de la Malmaison" after the rose grown in Empress Josephine's garden. It was brought to England in the 1860s, where it became the flower of fashion and a fixture in the grandest homes. In 1908, eighteen varieties of Malmaison were listed in a Glasgow nursery, all sought after for their distinctive fragrance of clove. Today Malmaison remains one of the most famous fragrances of Floris, the old English house of perfume. Nonetheless, only five Malmaisons remain in cultivation, some of which are still growing at the Royal Horticultural Society garden at Wisley.

The new cut carnations that developed in the florist industry in the 1950s and 1960s came in a wide range of colors and were available in abundance, but alas, had no fragrance. Carnations became so ubiquitous that they are now regarded with disdain. But it's time that we rediscover the beauty of these celebrated flowers with their finely ruffled petals. New fragrant varieties in subtle hues will certainly help start a carnation revival.

There are carnations in almost every color. Choose a few stems in deep magenta fringed with light pink for a dramatic summer arrangement or tuck a few blooms in varying shades of coral into a pretty cup for a charming addition to the tea tray (opposite).

Arranging Things   A Rhetoric of Object Placement   Koren

JOHN UPDIKE THE WOMEN WHO GOT AWAY   GREAT LOVES 20

IVAN TURGENEV FIRST LOVE   GREAT LOVES 7

How to tell the Birds from the Flowers   P

FRANÇOISE SAGAN BONJOUR TRISTESSE   GREAT LOVES 16

Olds   SATAN SAYS

The seventeenth-century Dutch painter Balthasar van der Ast painted some of the most exquisite striped carnations. A few solid pink blooms bring out the painterly quality of these white carnations with purple stripes.

THE NAMING OF NAMES ANNA PAVORD

NATURE DIARY

Tiger lilies come ablaze in late summer with their distinctive orange flowers decorated with black or dark red spots. Just a couple of stems of these fragrant blooms will make a graceful display in any home. OPPOSITE The wild carrot that grows rampant on roadsides, *Daucus carota*, is more commonly known as Queen Anne's lace, a host plant for black swallow-tail butterflies. Its umbels of tiny flowers sitting atop long, straight stalks exude an easy elegance when placed in a pretty glass vase.

Wild roses were blooming in the world long before the arrival of man. No other flower is more celebrated in the history of civilization than the rose. Since ancient times, its sumptuous flowers and heady scent have never ceased to capture the imagination of poets and mythmakers. Pink luscious blooms are paired with dark purple basil to create a dramatic and fragrant bouquet.

Poets through the ages have written rapturously about the rose, none more than the German Rainer Maria Rilke, who penned a sequence of poems in French dedicated to the flower. "Other flowers decorate the table that you transfigure," he wrote. Luscious yellow roses mixed with curly geranium leaves and feathery lady's mantle flowers bring a luminous elegance to the table. OPPOSITE A single bloom of the wine-red pincushion flower adds a light, summery touch to the library.

The influential photographer Edward Steichen had a love for delphinium, which he cultivated by the thousands on his farm in Connecticut. They were the subject of MoMA's first dedicated flower show, which featured both his plants and photographs of them. It's not difficult to appreciate these stately blue flowers that lend their elegance to any garden or home. OPPOSITE The last peonies of the season get top billing in this bouquet, with ninebark branches, pincushion flowers, and coral bell foliage and flowers.

Flowering maple, also known by its botanical name, *Abutilon*, is grown in mild climates, where its pendent bell-shaped flowers delight gardeners and hummingbirds alike. Mixed with the dramatic foliage of the purple-leaf Chinese fringe flower (*Loropelatum*), a profusion of coral-colored flowering maple adds a bright note to the music room. OPPOSITE The humble white pincushion flowers are given the royal treatment in a vintage blue and white pitcher.

A. H. Gale & Cº.

The passionflower got its name from sixteenth-century Christian missionaries in South America, to whom the flower symbolized various elements of the Crucifixion. Place these wondrous flowers where their pretty vines can trail freely.

OPPOSITE The Victorian art critic John Ruskin wrote that the poppy is "the most transparent and delicate of all the blossoms of the field." With petals like pastel-colored crepe papers on long, wavy stems, these flowers are as cheerful as a summer's day.

Bring home a taste of summer with a few branches dripping with juicy red currants. OPPOSITE Blueberries and Russian olive foliage set the stage for the dramatic red peonies in a centerpiece. Hydrangea and coral bell flowers and leaves round out the arrangement.

Nothing is more charming than a garden posy. Simply tuck a few stems of pink masterwort (*Astrantia major*) and lavender blooms with some lamb's ears foliage in a small vase and be charmed by the posy's unfussy loveliness. OPPOSITE Summer is the time of roses, so gather these perfumed beauties and mix them with spikes of mullein (*Verbascum x hybrida*) and dark coral bell leaves for a sweet bouquet.

The English diarist Samuel Pepys once wrote that the honeysuckle's "ivory bugles blow scent instead of sound." The trailing vines of honeysuckle make this arrangement of peonies, roses, blueberries, and coral bell leaves a sweet summer symphony.

The fluffy purple-pink plumes that appear after flowering on *Cotinus coggygria* resemble puffs of smoke, earning this popular garden plant its common name, smoke bush. Sturdy branches covered in a long-lasting, smoky haze bring the fulsome beauty of summer indoors.

Hydrangeas the color of the sky at sunset, streaked with shades of violet and pink, set the tenor of this rhapsody in blue, which also includes alliums, lavender, and honeywort (*Cerinthe major* 'Purpurascens').

Savor the last days of summer by combining blackberries on the vines with the first dahlias of the season in an arrangement that is evocative of the wild days of summer as well as the mellow mood of the coming autumn.

Spring

Summer

Autumn

Winter

"fruit ripening in stillness—Autumn suns
Smiling at eve upon the quiet sheaves"

JOHN KEATS, "Sonnet: After Dark Vapors Have Oppress'd Our Plains"

The season's glory is bound up in this arrangement of deep red dahlias, bright red Rose of Sharon seedpods, fiery viburnum leaves, and feathery willow myrtle foliage. OPPOSITE Crab apple fruits, ripened by the autumn sun, provide juicy treats for overwintering birds. Large branches of crab apple, laden with dark red fruits, lend an autumnal splendor in the home.

Celebrate the season of mellow fruitfulness with a bountiful harvest of Italian prune plums, one of the many varieties of the European plum that ripens later than the Japanese variety. OPPOSITE With delicate flowers borne on thin, wiry stems, Japanese anemones enliven the autumn garden, blooming profusely long after all the summer flowers have faded.

Dahlia *Dahlia*

DAHLIA flowers know the true meaning of variety. They come in the widest array of colors, sizes, and forms. Their blooms vary from half-inch pompons to more than ten-inch dinner-plate size, in every color except green, brown, and true blue. The ray florets (commonly mistaken as petals) on these luscious flowers might be spiky, wavy, wispy, round, or thin. There are officially eighteen types of dahlias, some of which are said to resemble water lily, cactus, peony, orchid, or anemone.

The original dahlias grew in the mountainous region of Mexico and were most likely single-flowered. In 1789 seeds sent from Mexico to the Botanical Garden of Madrid produced the first dahlia flowers in Europe. The new flower was named *Dahlia coccinea*, after the Swedish botanist Anders Dahl. From Madrid, seeds were sent to famous gardens in England and France. In a note to his wife in 1824, Lord Holland, whose librarian and gardener had succeeded in growing the dahlias from seeds sent by Lady Holland from Madrid, described the new flowers "as sweet as your smile, and in colour as bright as your cheek." Five years later, the garden writer John Loudon proclaimed the dahlia "the most fashionable flower in England."

In her famous garden at Malmaison, Empress Joséphine grew several varieties of dahlias in shades of red, yellow, and purple from seeds obtained in Mexico by the botanical explorer Friedrich Humboldt. The striking flower from the New World caught the imagination of European plant breeders with its prolific variation. In 1826 the Horticultural Society of London had a collection of sixty cultivars; in 1841 the list grew to more than 1,200. By the middle of the nineteenth century, the records show 3,000 cultivars, created by plant breeders all over Europe, including J. Wallner of Geneva, who cultivated the flower for more than fifty years and had a collection of 1,400 varieties.

The stunning colors and endlessly variable forms of the dahlia that flowers so generously from midsummer until frost have enchanted plant lovers since its introduction into the garden. The Dahlia Walk, planted at Bidduph Grange in Staffordshire in 1840 and restored recently, remains one of the most beautiful gardens devoted to dahlias. The long stepped path, framed by yew, is lined with compartments featuring different kinds of dahlias, highlighting their many ravishing colors and forms.

The only thing dahlia does not offer is a scent, which to some might be a fatal flaw. The poet Paul Verlaine, somewhat uncharitably, described it as a "hard-bosomed courtesan" around whom floats no aroma despite the lushness and opulence of her beauty.

OVERLEAF Sumptuous dahlias, foxgloves, and roses in autumn's mellow hues are combined with fragrant mountain mint and porcelain berries in cool tones to make up this extravagant bouquet, a celebration of the season's bounty.

Enjoy the cornucopia of autumn in an arrangement of pomegranates, rose hips, bronze fennel, pincushion flower seedpods, amaranth foliage, and dahlias. OPPOSITE Before the introduction of the repeat-blooming tea roses from China, the only rose to flower beyond summer was the 'Autumn Damask' rose. Praised by Virgil and Pliny, its beauty was unsurpassed and its fragrance legendary. Today, the rose's blooming season is prolonged with many autumn-flowering varieties. Cherish the last of the autumn roses in a romantic bouquet with voluptuous café-au-lait dahlias and the arching vines of clematis.

Dahlias come in a
blaze of colors and
settle easily into
any bouquet. Com-
bine red, orange,
and coral dahlias
with glossy abelia
and barberry foli-
age for an elegant
centerpiece.

Simply mix large dahlias in intense red with peachy-pink ones for a pretty arrangement in the bedroom. OPPOSITE The vibrantly colored zinnias are magnets for butterflies in the garden and flower prolifically from summer through fall. Bright yellow zinnias tinged with orange are highlighted with wine-red stonecrop and coral bell leaves for a carefree autumn bouquet.

Live Forever Elizabeth Peyton

In early autumn
the airy mustard-
color bronze fennel
flowers turn into
shades of copper
and bronze that
make a stunning
display. OPPOSITE
Café-au-lait
dahlias are among
the most ravishing
flowers in autumn.
Creamy blooms
lightly stained
with peachy-pink
overtones and
gently wavy petals,
these dinnerplate
dahlias make a
gorgeous bouquet
with burnished
blue hydrangea,
amaranth,
and crab apples.

Ornamental oregano has trailing stems of chartreuse bracts that change into shades of mauve and lilac. Gather them into a pretty little vase to enjoy their minty scent and gorgeous colors before the plant goes dormant with the first frost. OPPOSITE

As the summer fades and the sun casts lengthening shadows on the landscape, autumn foliage comes aflame in shades of red, purple, orange, and gold. The forsythia leaves turn yellow with a beguiling purple tinge.

Terenzio **The Collected Writings of Robert Motherwell**

Chrysanthemum *Chrysanthemum*

CHRYSANTHEMUM is a flower of ancient lineage. In cultivation two thousand years ago in China, it held the lofty status as one of the "Four Gentlemen" in floral symbolism. Also called the Four Noble Ones or Four Friends, the plum blossom, orchids, bamboo, and chrysanthemum represented loftiness, righteousness, modesty, and purity and were regularly featured in Chinese painting.

In Japan, the chrysanthemum's cultivation dates back over one thousand years. The imperial family crest bears the symbol of the sixteen-petaled flower. This symbol of longevity, dignity, and nobility was frequently used as a decorative motif in Japanese pottery, porcelain, lacquer ware, and textiles. In 910, the Emperor Uda instituted the first Chrysanthemum Festival in the gardens of the imperial residence, and it remains one of the five ancient sacred festivals of the country.

Chrysanthemum was introduced into Holland in 1688 but was not widely cultivated in Europe until the nineteenth century, when the Royal Horticultural Society of London dispatched plant collectors to China and Japan to bring back new varieties. Growers both in France and England also cultivated new forms and colors from seedlings. In 1859, at his retirement, the great English chrysanthemum grower John Salter had a collection of two thousand varieties. Annual exhibitions in various parts of England introduced the novelties—with such poetic names as Starry Purple, Quilled Lilac, and Curled Blush—to an appreciative public, and the chrysanthemum's fame spread far and wide.

Popular appreciation made the hardy chrysanthemum a cottage garden favorite and a staple of cut flowers in the florist trade. By the twentieth century, the noble chrysanthemum, inelegantly dubbed the "mum," had become ubiquitous and common. Today, literally thousands of different chrysanthemums are available all year round, in every color, size, and shape. Their forms range from simple daisy-like to buttons and pompons. The U.S. National Chrysanthemum Society lists thirteen official bloom forms. Recent efforts are being made to bring back the older, more elegant varieties and restore the chrysanthemum's reputation to its former glory.

From palace to cottage, the chrysanthemum is a flower of great antiquity. It is to autumn what the rose is to summer. Many cultivars bear flowers the colors of autumn: bronzy orange, mauve, russet, and copper. In the long years of its existence, there have been a multitude of changes to its character and form, but the chrysanthemum remains a jewel in the autumn garden.

Spider chrysanthemums in vivid chartreuse look positively regal in a vintage blue-and-white ceramic vase, while russet-colored chrysanthemums mix well with cosmos, rose hips, and willow myrtle leaves (opposite).

Chrysanthemums come in many colors, but the yellow chrysanthemum makes a lasting impression. To Confucian scholars in ancient China, it symbolizes the promise of loyalty to the ruler. In her poem "The Coming of the Chrysanthemum" the American poet Bernece Rodman wrote, "forth from October's shade she silently came, opening all her glowing golden rays, to brighten and hallow the late autumnal days." Make room for these golden beauties to brighten your home. OPPOSITE Chrysanthemums in various forms and shades of mauve, from the darkest plum to pale lilac, are gathered for an elegant bouquet.

Poets from east to west have found meaning in the ancient chrysanthemum. Thomas Hardy, in his poem "The Last Chrysanthemum," saw the late autumnal flower, its beauty a "lonely thing," as "one mask of many worn by the Great Face behind." The Korean poet Seo Jung Ju found intimation of the cosmic principle of life in the contemplation of a single chrysanthemum. OPPOSITE Amaranth embodies the rich jewel tones of autumn with its dramatic ropes of ruby-red flowers accompanied by brilliantly hot-colored leaves that run the gamut from jade green to burnished gold and garnet red. Purple coneflower seed heads, a magnet for gold finches and other birdsongs, add a textural accent to this stunning arrangement.

Glossy abelia, a native of Eastern Asia and Mexico, has a long flowering season and is coveted by butterflies. The diminutive bell-shaped and pink-tinged abelia flowers, borne profusely on graceful arching stems from June until frost, are fragrant and long lasting as cut flowers. Mixed with bold hippeastrum and feathery grass, glossy abelia makes a voluminous arrangement in early autumn. OPPOSITE Chinese pistachio trees have spectacular autumn foliage. Bring home a few branches to watch the leaves change colors from bright green to yellow, then coppery bronze to dark maroon, complemented by tiny, bright red fruits.

Oakleaf hydrangea takes on gorgeous colors in the softening light of autumn, the panicles of blooms turning chartreuse and dusty pink, while the beautiful large leaves darken to a deep burgundy. OPPOSITE The pincushion flower seedpod is a sculptural marvel. Held on a long, elegant stem is an ornate ball of intricately striped cups, each holding precariously in its center a dark wiry star. These seedpods make a striking autumn display that is also long lasting.

Roses are generous plants, providing us with beautiful flowers that, once spent, turn into luscious hips in shades of red, orange, and purple. Bring these lovely rose hips home to make tea or put them in a vase to appreciate their graceful beauty.

Spring
Summer
Autumn

Winter

"Silent, and soft, and slow
Descends the snow"

HENRY WORDSWORTH LONGFELLOW, "Snow-Flakes"

Without the distraction of flowers and foliage, the trees in winter take on a sculptural quality, their bare branches etching infinite patterns against the sky. The corkscrew hazel has wonderfully curled and twisted branches that are best appreciated after all the leaves have dropped. It is also known as Harry Lauder's Walking Stick, after a Scottish musician who entertained American soldiers during World War I.

Citrus is the perfect remedy for winter blues, bringing a flash of color and fresh scent. Tiny orange kumquats are combined with paper whites, dark berries of mature English ivy, and lacy ferns to make a lovely and fragrant bouquet. OPPOSITE The olive, mentioned in ancient texts from Homer and Horace to the Bible and the Quran, is a native of the Mediterranean region but is now grown all over the world, including in California. The olive tree can live for centuries, its evergreen branches bearing fruit a welcoming sight in winter.

Sculptural, spreading branches of cedar, cypress, and eucalyptus set the stage for this sumptuous holiday arrangement with bold, pink-flushed hippeastrum blooms and delicate, green hellebores.

Hippeastrum, often mistakenly called amaryllis, are large and striking flowers grown indoors from bulbs. With colors ranging from pure white, pale pink, and coral to outrageous orange and deep velvet red (opposite), these dazzling flowers brighten a winter window and enliven the dull days of the season.

The J. Paul Getty Museum, Los Angeles

The bittersweet vines produce orange-red berries enveloped in bright yellow skin that persist through the winter. A mass of tangled vines with their berries makes a long-lasting and carefree winter arrangement.

The tradition of bringing evergreen boughs into the home during the barren months of winter originated with the ancient Nordic peoples who inhabited the frigid, wind-swept forests of northern Europe. A beautiful and fragrant arrangement of holly, fir, spruce, and Japanese cedar, gathered simply into a bucket, will dispel the gloom of winter days and fill the house with its scent. OPPOSITE The spring snow-flake, *Leucojum vernum*, a sweet bellflower with sea-green markings on pristine white petals, blooms with a vaguely violet scent as soon as the snow melts in the woodlands and continues through early spring.

Christmas Rose *Helleborus*

THE GENUS *HELLEBORUS* includes about twenty different species that bloom from Christmas to Easter. Found in much of Europe and part of Asia, *Helleborus* is prized in the garden for its sumptuous winter flowers, commonly known as the Christmas rose, Lenten rose, snow rose, or hellebore. For such a wondrous flower, it has a name that hints at a darker side. The Latin name comes from the Greek *Helleborus*, a combination of *helein*, to kill, and *bora*, food—meaning food that kills. The plant contains alkaloids and other chemicals that can lead to poisoning if ingested in large quantities.

In cultivation since ancient time, the hellebore is mentioned as a drug, purgative, and poison in Theophrastus's botanical treatise more than 2,200 years ago. Pliny the Elder also wrote about the hellebore in his encyclopedic work *Naturalis Historia*, citing its use in remedies to relieve various ailments. Medieval herbalists used the plant, and it was cultivated for medicinal purposes in monastery gardens.

Hellebores are undoubtedly the stars of the winter garden. Their flowers resemble the wild rose, with hauntingly beautiful colors in smoky purples and pinks to pure white. What looks like petals on the gracious hellebores are actually sepals. Unlike the petals in most flowers, the sepals persist long after fertilization and never really fall off. Except for the dark-hued blooms, they simply change colors, often turning green as photosynthetic activity increases. So the flowers last for months, changing their hues over time. Dedicated gardeners and nurserymen are constantly hybridizing different species to create a tantalizing range of flower shape, size, and color—including some with delicate speckles or a narrow edge of a darker color, an effect known as picotee. As cut flowers, they are not fond of overheated rooms but otherwise are especially long lasting.

A feature of the English cottage garden, the Christmas rose (*Helleborus niger*) bears its cheerful white flowers that age to pink in the bleakest months of winter. Writers and poets through the ages have marveled at the sight of it blooming under a blanket of snow. In his epic work *The Loves of Plants*, the great polymath Erasmus Darwin (grandfather of Charles Darwin) summons up the spell that the hellebore casts on all men:

> "Bright as the silvery plume, or pearly shell,
> The snow white rose or lily's virgin bell,
> The fair helleborus attractive shone,
> Warmed every sage and every shepherd won."

Hellebores range in color from pure white to virtually black, with almost every shade of green, yellow, pink, and purple in between. Cluster hellebores in different colors, each in its own vase, or mix them all together in one container for an inviting winter arrangement.

Rhododendron may be prized for its showy flowers in the spring, but in winter, its evergreen foliage—whorls of glossy green leaves on spreading branches—is handsome enough to bring indoors. OPPOSITE The sophisticated beauty of dark, smoky purple hellebores is the perfect antidote for a bleak, cold day.

Winterberry, unlike other hollies, is deciduous and therefore sheds its leaves in winter, leaving its berries to cover the bare branches with their bright color. Most winterberries are red, but the cultivar 'Winter Gold' offers fruits in an unusual golden orange. OPPOSITE Andromeda, *Pieris japonica*, produces showy, pendulous clusters of sweetly scented white or pink flowers in late winter. Look at the papery bells up close to appreciate the subtly changing colors as they bloom.

Flowering Quince *Chaenomeles*

THE FLOWERING QUINCE is known for its delicately beautiful flowers that bloom on bare twigs in late winter through spring. Native to the mountain woodlands of China, Japan, and Korea, the plant has been in cultivation for centuries, its flowers used to decorate houses, and its fragrant fruits brought indoors to perfume rooms. Since the sixteenth century, flowering quince has frequently appeared in Chinese and Japanese paintings, and the exquisite blooms on its thorny and leafless stems are evocative of Asian art and Japanese textiles. The dramatic and sculptural quality of the plant remains a popular motif in chinoiserie decorative arts. One of the most iconic chinoiserie wallpapers today is the Flowering Quince by the fabric manufacturer Clarence House. Created by the company's art director Kazumi Yoshida, the design is based on the fabric of an antique kimono. This popular wallpaper can be seen covering the walls of stylish homes from Hollywood to New York City, a testament to the aesthetic appeal of the flowering quince.

Most of the flowering quince in cultivation today comes from two separate species, the Chinese quince, *Chaenomeles speciosa*, and the Japanese quince, *Chaenomeles japonica*. The Chinese quince arrived in Europe in 1796 and the Japanese species made its appearance there nearly a century later, in 1869. Out of the two species, more than five hundred varieties have been bred, ranging from pure white to the palest of pinks, coral, flame, and the darkest scarlet.

For Chinese Americans, the flowering quince has become the symbolic flower of the Chinese New Year, as the flowering peach, so favored in southern China for the occasion, blooms much later. In late January or early February, vendors in Chinatown in San Francisco and New York offer large branches of flowering quince full of tight buds. For the Chinese and other East Asians who celebrate the lunar new year, it is a tradition to bring flowering branches into one's home in the hope that the buds will open precisely on New Year's Day, signifying prosperity for the coming year. The flowering quince's beguiling blossoms, painted pale pink or deep crimson against the dark, leafless branch, accompany the sense of excitement and anticipation of this special time of year. Bound up in the delicate petals, whose beauty is as fragile and fleeting as a whisper, is all the hope and optimism of the beginning of a journey, the fresh start of the new year.

Bring home an armful of flowering quince branches and watch the delicate buds unfold into exquisitely beautiful blossoms that herald the lunar new year.

A bare branch of flowering quince smeared in coral blossoms brings a spark of beauty to a dreary day in February. OPPOSITE The saying goes, "Three more snows after the forsythia blooms," so when these tiny golden bell flowers burst open in showy exuberance, it's a sign that winter is in retreat. Branches of forsythia with buds can be cut as early as January to be forced indoors.

Witch hazel is one of the earliest-blooming flowers of the year, bringing a much-needed burst of color into the winter landscape. The spidery petals unfurl in thick clusters along leafless stems, their bright red and yellow colors standing out brilliantly against the snow. Witch hazel makes long-lasting cut flowers with a spicy scent to perfume the air.

In China the flowering plum trees (some dating back more than one thousand years) begin blooming in the bitter winter and continue into early spring. The dainty plum blossoms, colored in white, rose, or deep red, are a beloved subject of Asian paintings, symbolizing hope and fortitude. The Japanese celebrate the flowering of plum blossoms with festivals around the country.

A carpet of lilac-flame crocus blooming merrily—sometimes while snow is still on the ground—is a heart-warming sight on wintry days. Cut crocus flowers do not last long, but these venturous blooms are a cheer-ful reminder that spring is on its way. OPPOSITE Pussy willow bears soft, fluffy silver flowers that provide a cru-cial early source of nectar and pollen for foraging bees. Indoors, the tall stems of pussy wil-lows make a striking arrangement that will last for weeks.

Caring for Cut Flowers

UNLIKE THE RELUCTANT SCHOLAR Biron in Shakespeare's *Love's Labour's Lost*, who no more desires a rose at Christmas "than wish a snow in May's new-fangled mirth," we are accustomed to having roses any day of the year. In addition to roses, many other flowers are readily available out of season, including peonies, carnations, and chrysanthemums. Roses or peonies offered at the florists in December are likely to have been harvested in South America or New Zealand and flown to the Netherlands for auction before being repacked and sent to North America. But in recent years, concerns for the global environment and the rising costs of freight have led to an increasing demand for locally sourced flowers. Without the strict packing requirements for long-distance transport that favor straight and stiff commercially bred flowers, local growers can deliver flowers with more organic attributes, such as curving stems and bent flower heads, which are important aesthetic criteria for a more naturalistic arrangement.

Today you can find fresh, local, and seasonal blooms at farmers' markets, farm stands, pick-your-own flower farms, backyard gardens, and even roadsides. Some urban greengrocers also offer seasonal flowers along with their produce. CookBook, a greengrocer in the Los Angeles neighborhood of Echo Park, sells local, organic flowers grown at the North Hollywood High School garden. Don't be afraid to ask the vendors at the farmers' market or your local florists for your favorite locally grown flowers if you don't see them on offer. In addition to flowers, many garden plants with interesting foliage like coral bells (*Heuchera*) and lamb's ears (*Stachys byzantine*) add appealing textures to a floral arrangement. Even if you don't have a garden, these can be grown in pots on a sunny window or fire escape.

Whether you cut your own flowers or buy them, here are some simple rules to ensure their longevity in your home:

- If you are lucky enough to be able to take cuttings from your own garden, it is best to cut flowers early in the morning or in the evening.

- Be sure not to select flowers that are too open or buds that are unripe. Pick fully developed buds that show good color, indicating their ripeness.

- Minimize the time flowers spend out of water. If you purchased your flowers, unwrap them as soon as you get home.

- Cut the end of the stems on the diagonal with sharp scissors or a knife. This will allow maximum exposure to water. Contrary to popular belief, smashing the ends of woody stems actually damages the vascular system of the branches and therefore inhibits water absorption.

- Remove all unnecessary foliage, especially that below the water line, to prevent bacteria growth. Eliminating most of the foliage also allows more water to go directly to the flower heads.

- Condition the flowers by standing them in deep lukewarm water in a cool place for a few hours before arranging them. This will allow the cut flowers to drink as much water as possible and regain their energy and strength.

- Clean your vases thoroughly and dry them to ensure that they are free of bacteria before filling them with water.

- Fill your vase with lukewarm water, which provides more oxygen than cold water, helping the flowers last longer.

- Avoid placing flowers in direct sunlight, near a heat source, or in a drafty spot. Most flowers, with the possible exception of the tropical ones, prefer a cool room.

- Floral food packages that come with the florist's bouquets contain glucose to feed the flowers and disinfectant to keep the water clean. By changing the water frequently, you can eliminate the need for disinfectant. Sugar can be added to the water as additional energy for the flowers, but often this is not necessary.

The longevity of cut flowers varies greatly, but most fresh-cut flowers should last three to eight days. Fragrant flowers tend to be more short-lived since much of their energy is devoted to producing scent. Specially bred florist flowers may last longer than their more fragile garden counterparts if they have been properly conditioned during transport.

NOTES ON SPECIFIC VARIETIES

- Anemone and tulips continue to grow in water and are thirsty drinkers. Tulips will even move toward the light, a fact that should be taken into account when making your arrangement. Make sure you change the water regularly and fill up the vase well.

- Hydrangeas, lilacs, and viburnum drink from their blooms as well as their stems and therefore should be gently sprayed each day with water to keep their freshness.

- Carnations have thick nodes along the stem. Always cut between the nodes to allow water to penetrate the stem. Carnations have an exceptionally long vase life, lasting up to two weeks or more if kept in the right condition.

- Chrysanthemums are also especially long lasting as cut flowers, with a vase life of up to two weeks. However, their foliage can die before the flowers do so make sure to remove any yellow leaves.

- Daffodils exude a clear sap that can kill other flowers. Condition them separately in water for at least a few hours before adding them to any arrangements.

- Cut gardenias tend to turn brown quickly. To prevent this, spray the flower with a fine mist of lemon juice. The oil from your hands will also discolor the bloom, so wet your hands before handling gardenias. Change the vase water every day.

- Refresh droopy hydrangeas by submerging them head down in cool water for twenty minutes to an hour, allowing their petals to firm up again. Recut their stems at an angle before placing them back in the arrangement. Hydrangea flowers are fast drinkers so make sure to refill the vase water frequently.

- Irises are especially susceptible to bacteria so it is essential to dispose of any iris that's past its prime to avoid infecting other flowers in the arrangement.

- Most poppies from the florists are singed at the end of the stems to keep them from exuding a milky sap. Once you have made a new cut at home, resinge the stem on an open flame.

- The fluffy white blossoms on pussy willow stems will develop bright yellow pollen or yellow-green carpels, depending on the sex of the flower, if you put water in the vase. To keep the furry-looking flowers unchanged, don't put water in the vase. The flowers will remain in the same state as when they first burst from their buds for a couple of weeks until they dry out.

Finally, a note of caution: many flowers and plants—azalea, clematis, carnation, chrysanthemum, foxglove, hellebore, holly, lily, and bittersweet, among others—are toxic to animals so be sure to keep them away from your pets. Foxglove is also known to cause severe allergic reaction for some people, so handle it with care if you are not sure.

TOOLS FOR FLOWER ARRANGING

CLIPPERS The most important tool for flower arranging is a sharp pair of clippers or scissors to ensure a clean cut. Dull blades can damage the stems and inhibit water absorption. For cutting woody-stemmed blooms, it might be preferable to use floral knives. However, a sharp pair of floral clippers or scissors can handle most stems.

FLOWER FROGS Flower frogs, made popular in the 1920s and '30s, are a great way to hold your flowers in place and an absolute necessity in making arrangements in shallow bowls. They come in a variety of designs and styles to fit different types of vases. The metal flower frogs have needles or pins attached to a metal base. They are usually round, but other shapes are also available. Flower frogs can also be made of glass, with holes to support the placement of the flower stems.

FLORAL WIRE Other useful items include floral wire to hold the stems, as well as raffia and ribbons, used for tying and adding a decorative flourish to the bouquet.

NOTE: The use of floral foams is strongly discouraged. These flower holders were invented in 1954 and replaced flower frogs in much of the florist industry. However, floral foam is made of non-biodegradable plastic and contains toxic materials that can cause irritation to the eyes and skin.

Vases

IN HIS 1880 LECTURE ENTITLED *Beauty of Life*, William Morris, the leading exponent of the Arts and Crafts movement, listed among the "simple necessities" that ought to furnish a room, "a vase or two to put flowers in, which latter you must have sometimes, especially if you live in a town." In his case, the vase was likely to be a simple jug, but throughout history, flower vases have come in many forms and materials. The ancient Egyptians favored basins, or wide-mouthed vessels with tapering pedestals. The ancient Greeks had their cornucopias. In Renaissance Italy, there were beautiful vases in marble, maiolica, heavy Venetian glass, and bronze.

In Dutch and Flemish seventeenth-century flower paintings, sumptuous bouquets were tucked into beautifully shaped glass vessels, classic terra-cotta urns, or blue and white Chinese porcelain, a product of the lively trade with the East. Factories around Delft in the Netherlands developed a method of using tin-glazed earthenware to reproduce the look of blue and white porcelain from Kangxi in China, and Delftware vases inspired by Chinese originals were widely popular all over Europe. The Delft flower holders came in many shapes, such as tall baluster vases, urns, and pyramids of varying heights with individual reservoirs ascending from a base. The pyramid and baluster vases often had spouts for individual flowers and were favored by Princess Mary, wife of Prince William II of Orange, for her beloved bouquets at Het Loo Palace.

King Louis XIV's mistress, Mme de Montespan, preferred her flowers arranged in silver baskets and placed on the floor throughout the palace at Versailles. The more efficient-minded Gertrude Jekyll, one of England's most influential garden designers and an authority on floral decoration, bemoaned the impracticality of the tall trumpet-shape vases that were popular at the beginning of the twentieth century and set about to design a series of plain glass vessels with wider bases to facilitate better water absorption. These simple vases, named Munstead Flower Glasses after Jekyll's famous garden, were a huge hit at the time.

Today there is a multitude of vases from which to choose. It is ideal to have a selection of vessels in various shapes and heights to accommodate different arrangements. Apart from traditional vases, a number of ordinary objects of everyday use can be pressed into service as flower vases:

- Large vintage apothecary bottles make great containers for tall flowering branches.

- Small, hand-tied posies sit beautifully in mugs or cups.

- Old tin cans with interesting graphics make perfect vessels for informal bouquets. You can even paint tin cans in your favorite colors to make fresh and modern vases.

- Small soda bottles and beautiful etched glasses make great bud vases. Gather a few together in different heights to make a lovely grouping.

- Mason jars and old milk bottles lend a rustic air to an arrangement of wildflowers.

- Footed compote bowls work well for more formal bouquets with trailing stems or vines.

Whatever you choose to use as a vase, make sure it is the right proportion and color for the flowers. Except for tall flowering branches, a general rule of thumb is to make your flowers about one and a half times the height of the container. Just keep in mind that the arrangement shouldn't look top-heavy or as if it will topple over.

How to Arrange Flowers

FOR AS LONG AS PEOPLE HAVE BEEN USING FLOWERS to decorate, there have been many styles of floral arrangements. In the ancient world, the Greeks wove flowers into wreaths and garlands, while the Egyptians preferred formal, highly stylized designs in vases. The Byzantine bouquets were similarly decorous, strictly symmetrical compositions of flowers and fruits arranged into a cone shape. In the Baroque period, floral arrangements became more flamboyant, typically masses of many different kinds of flowers in an increasingly asymmetrical style. During this period English painter William Hogarth introduced the sweeping S-curve design that remains popular today. By the late nineteenth century, the Victorian English favored more natural, light, and graceful compositions of old-fashioned garden flowers mixed loosely with foliage and grasses. The Arts and Crafts movement rebelled against fussiness and advocated a more simplified way of displaying flowers in the home, which eventually led to the Edwardian fashion of single-flower arrangements, strictly one kind of flower per vase, sometimes with asparagus fern as an added element. In the 1920s Constance Spry, a teacher who became an influential floral designer, turned the tide back in favor of the "mixed bunches," as she called her pioneering arrangements. She also popularized the use of such unusual plant materials as ornamental kale, berries, and vegetables.

The most profound legacy that Constance Spry left on the art of floral design is her emphasis on understanding the nature of plants and flowers. A keen gardener, she had a deep appreciation of the intrinsic beauty of plants and flowers, which she sought to emphasize in her arrangements. In one of her last lectures, given in Australia in 1959, she said, "Let the flowers remind you of how they looked when growing." This is sensible advice. To show flowers to their best advantage, it makes perfect sense to appreciate their natural attributes, like the scalloped edges of a geranium leaf or the wavy bend of a poppy stem. Part of the enduring appeal of seventeenth-century Dutch flower paintings is the depiction of the exquisite details and graceful gestures of flowers: the delicate ruffles on carnations, the unfurling petals of half-open roses, or the elegant curve of tulip stems.

Get in touch with nature to see flowers and plants in a meaningful way. If you are not a gardener, go for walks in the woods or visit public gardens to discover the variety of plants and flowers that grow in your area. Seeing plant combinations in nature will give you an idea of which flowers might look good together in an arrangement. Look at a plant closely and it will reveal its secrets. The foxglove, for example, has intricate markings that form a path inside the flower from the bottom of the opening through its tunnel shape, right up to the nectar. These seemingly decorative markings in fact have a very practical function: they help bumble bees, foxglove's main pollinators, find their way inside the flower's tunnel to get the nectar. Such is the wondrous beauty of foxglove. Place your arrangement of foxgloves on a desk or someplace where you will appreciate these tiny details. Likewise, put fragrant flowers like a damask rose or honeysuckle in a place where you will be able to enjoy their scents.

The arrangements in these pages strive to capture the natural gestures of plants and flowers. Whether it's a large mixed arrangement or a more intimate display of a single stem or two, the aim is invariably to evoke the beauty and romance inherent in flowers. Focus on the particular offerings of each season, from blossoming branches in spring and vivid colored flowers in summer, to autumn's bronzed foliage and winter's evergreen. Be imaginative with your use of plant materials. Flowers come in myriad forms and colors, so find the ones that appeal most to you. Pick your favorite colors and do not hesitate to experiment, mixing them in a way that is most pleasing to you. Make a bouquet of one kind of flowers in varying shades of the same hue or an arrangement of different flowers in the same color. Take advantage of the rich variety of foliage from the garden or your houseplants to incorporate different textures, sizes, and shapes into your bouquet. Fruits, seedpods, and herbs are all uniquely beautiful and deserve to be brought indoors for your up-close appreciation.

Floral arrangements need not be a formal affair. Tuck a handful of wildflowers into a simple glass jar, as people have done for centuries, and you have an enchanting floral display for your home. Alternatively, you can be inspired by the Edwardian English and make an arrangement of various flowers by keeping each type in a separate vase and grouping them together. Vary the height of each vase for a more interesting composition. Resist the temptation to put too many kinds of flowers in one arrangement. Be extravagant and make room for large branches of spring blossoms or autumn fruits in beautiful vessels. Nothing is more elegant than a single stem or vine in a pretty bud vase. For those occasions that call for a more formal floral presentation, there is a simple way to achieve a naturalistic, graceful arrangement.

FABULOUS ARRANGEMENTS IN THREE EASY STEPS

The building blocks of a beautiful arrangement consist of three simple elements: a basic structure, points of focus, and a gestural finish.

1. **BASIC STRUCTURE:** Establish the fundamental shape of the arrangement using branches and greenery. A slightly asymmetrical shape is best for a natural look. If possible, use a flower frog to place branches and stems in the desired position.

2. **POINTS OF FOCUS:** Position the flowers that make up the main attraction of the arrangement. Cut the stems of flowers in various heights to place them at different levels of the composition. Make sure these flowers are clearly visible within the arrangement.

3. **GESTURAL FINISH:** Add wispy elements, such as feathery flowers, arching vines, and delicate foliage to create sweeping and gestural lines. These final elements should give the arrangement a sense of movement, spontaneity, and flourish.

Keep the arrangement airy and loose for a naturalistic feel. The flowers and foliage should retain as much of their natural habit as possible, rather than looking forced and stiff. The less contrived an arrangement looks, the more you will notice the beauty of the individual flowers.

SPRING

INGREDIENTS (left to right) Akeba foliage, white hyacinth, pink anemone, pink and white tulip, pink jasmine, and corydalis foliage

BASIC STRUCTURE

POINTS OF FOCUS

GESTURAL FINISH

SUMMER

INGREDIENTS (left to right) Pincushion flower, coral bell flower, peony, coral bell foliage, ninebark flower and foliage

BASIC STRUCTURE

POINTS OF FOCUS

GESTURAL FINISH

AUTUMN

INGREDIENTS (left to right) Bronze fennel, amaranth, pomegranates, dahlias, rose hips, and pincushion flower seed pods

BASIC STRUCTURE

POINTS OF FOCUS

GESTURAL FINISH

WINTER

INGREDIENTS (left to right) Eucalyptus buds and pods, cypress foliage, begonia leaves, hellebores, and andromeda flowers

BASIC STRUCTURE

POINTS OF FOCUS

GESTURAL FINISH

Plant Calendar

"all things keep
Time with the season"

THOMAS CAREW, "The Spring"

Plant Calendar / *Spring*

SPRING offers the most spectacular blossoms and delicate flowering bulbs. The return of spring flowers is always a welcome sight after a long winter, and most flowering trees oblige by blooming profusely before the leaves appear. Large branches of flowering cherry, crab apple, lilac, and dogwood can be found at farmers' markets. Brightly colored bunches of daffodils, tulips, and hyacinths also make their appearance at the markets this time of year.

FLOWERING BRANCHES

Azalea
Rhododendron spp.
Blooms early spring

Cherry blossom
Prunus spp.
Blooms early spring

Crab apple
Malus spp.
Blooms early spring

Dogwood
Cornus florida
Blooms early spring

Eastern redbud
Cercis canandensis
Blooms early spring

Hawthorn
Craetagus spp.
Blooms early spring

Kousa dogwood
Cornus kousa
Blooms late spring

Lilac
Syringa vulgaris
Blooms early
to mid-spring

Mountain laurel
Kalmia latifolia
Blooms late spring

Rhododendron
Rhododendron hybrids
Blooms mid-spring

Saucer magnolia
Magnolia soulangeana
Blooms early spring

Spirea
Spiraea thunbergii
Blooms early spring

Star magnolia
Magnolia stellata
Blooms early spring

Sweet bay magnolia
Magnolia virginiana
Blooms late spring into summer

FLOWERS

Anemone
Anemone coronaria
Blooms mid- to late spring

Bachelor's button
Centaurea cyanus
Blooms spring and summer

Bleeding heart
Dicentra spectabilis
Blooms early spring

Camellia
Camellia japonica
Blooms early spring

Columbine
Aquilegia vulgaris
Blooms late spring to mid-summer

Crown imperial
Fritillaria imperialis
Blooms mid-spring

Daffodil
Narcissus
Blooms early spring

Daphne
Daphne x burwoodii
Fragrant, light pink flower, blooms mid- to late spring

Fritillary
Fritillaria meleagris
Blooms early spring

Grape hyacinth
Muscari armeniacum
Blooms early spring

Hyacinth
Hyacinthus orientalis
Blooms early spring

Herbaceous peony
Paeonia lactiflora
Blooms late spring
into early summer

Iris
Iris hollandica
Blooms mid- to late spring

Lily of the valley
Convallaria majalis
Blooms mid-spring

Ornamental Onion
Allium
Blooms from late spring
through summer

Pansy
Viola x wittrockiana
Blooms early spring and
from late autumn into winter

Persian fritillary
Fritillaria persica
Blooms early to mid-spring

Pink jasmine
Jasminum polyanthum
Blooms early spring
through summer

Ranunculus
Ranunculus
Blooms spring to summer

Siberian squill
Scilla siberica
Small blue flower, blooms
early spring

Solomon's seal
Polygonatum odoratum
Blooms early spring

Star of Bethlehem
Ornithogalum balansae
Very long-lasting cut flower,
blooms mid-spring

Sweet William
Dianthus barbatus
Blooms late spring

Tree peony
Paeonia suffruticosa
Blooms mid- to late spring

Tulip
Tulipa hybrids
Blooms early spring

Weigela
Weigela florida
Blooms mid-spring into
summer; some cultivars
bloom into autumn

Plant Calendar / *Summer*

SUMMER flowers are the most colorful. There are blooms ranging from the deepest red and darkest purple to shades of blue, yellow, and pink. Summer is also the time for the most canonical flowers—such as roses and peonies—as well as the humble wildflowers like Queen Anne's lace. Herbs and colorful berries are also thrown into the mix. Beautiful foliage of tender plants like begonia and coleus can add another layer of interest to any bouquet.

FLOWERS

Astilbe
Astilbe x arendsii
Blooms in early summer

Carnation
Dianthus caryophyllus
Blooms all summer

Clematis
Clematis hybrida
Blooms late spring and early summer to autumn

Coneflower
Echinacea purpurea
Blooms late summer to early autumn

Cosmos
Cosmos bipinnatus
Blooms in summer through autumn

Delphinium
Delphinium cultivars
Blooms all summer

Foxglove
Digitalis purpurea
Blooms early summer

Hollyhock
Alcea rosea
Blooms early to late summer

Honeysuckle
Lonicera sp
Blooms spring into autumn

Hydrangea
Hydrangea macrophylla, H. paniculata, H. arborescens
Blooms all summer into autumn

Lady's mantle
Achemillla mollis
Airy flowers in summer.

Lily
Lilium spp.
Large range of varieties blooming from mid to late summer

Masterwort
Astrantia major
Blooms early summer into early autumn

Nasturtium
Tropaeolum majus
Blooms all summer into autumn

Passionflower
Passiflora incarnata
Blooms in spring and summer

Phlox
Phlox paniculata
Blooms mid-summer to mid-autumn

Poppy
Papaver spp.
Blooms spring to summer

Purple coneflower
Echinacea purpurea
Blooms mid-summer until frost

Queen Anne's lace, aka wild carrot
Daucus Carota
Blooms summer into autumn

Rose
Rosa spp. & hybrids
Blooms late spring, early summer into autumn

Scabiosa/Pincushion flower
Scabiosa atropurpurea
Blooms summer until frost

Sea holly
Eryngium
Spiky blue flowers bloom mid- to late summer.

Smoke bush
Cotinus coggygria
Blooms in summer

Snapdragon
Antirrhinum majus
Mid- to late summer

Sweetpea
Lathyrus odoratus
Blooms all summer

Wild garlic
Tulbaghia violacea
Delicate, pale pink flowers early summer into autumn

Zinnia
Zinnia elegans
Blooms summer through autumn

HERB

Basil
Ocinum basilicum
Blooms in mid-summer

Lavender
Lavandula
Blooms all summer

Mountain mint
Pycnanthemum
Blooms summer into early autumn

Oregano
Origanum

Sage
Salvia officinalis

FOLIAGE

Begonia
Begonia
Flowers in summer. Foliage comes in a range of colors, some variegated or spotted.

Coleus
Coleus x hybridus
Variegated foliage mostly with dark red and plum colors

Coral bells
Heuchera sanguinea
Colorful foliage ranges from yellows, reds, and purples.

Corydalis
Corydalis
Delicate fern-like foliage

Lamb's Ear
Stachys byzantina
Fuzzy silver-white foliage

Oxalis
Oxalis
Clover-like leaves in light green or dark purple

Russian olive
Eleagnus Augustifolia
Branches of silvery green leaves make a lovely arrangement alone or add nicely to a mixed bouquet.

FRUIT

Blackberry
Rubus villosus

Blueberry
Vaccinium spp.

Fig
Ficus carica

Red currant
Ribes spp.

Plant Calendar / *Autumn*

In **AUTUMN** the focus shifts from flowers to fruit and seed heads. Sumptuous dahlias and chrysanthemums are the mainstay for fall arrangements, but the intensely colorful foliage of maples, burning bush, and other trees make striking additions to the home. Pomegranates, persimmons, and crab apples come in autumnal hues of orange and red, emphasizing the cornucopia of the season.

FLOWERS

Amaranth
Amaranthus
Foliage ranges from purple and red to gold. Flowers from summer until frost

Aster
Aster spp.
Blooms from late summer into autumn

Black-eyed Susan
Rudbeckia hirta
Blooms late summer into autumn

Bronze fennel
Foeniculum vulgare
Blooms from spring into early autumn

Cosmos
Cosmos spp.
Flowers from spring to early autumn

Chrysanthemum
Chrysanthemum morifolium
Blooms late summer through autumn

Dahlia
Dahlia
Blooms late summer through autumn

Glossy abelia
Abelia x grandiflora
Flowers from early summer to frost

Japanese anemone
Anemone x hybrida
Blooms late summer into autumn

Mexican orange blossom
Choisya ternata
White fragrant flowers bloom in spring and again in autumn.

Oakleaf hydrangea
Hydrangea quercifolia
Blooms mid-summer into autumn, when foliage turns deep burgundy

Queen Anne's lace
Daucus carota
Blooms summer into autumn

Stonecrop
Sedum
Flowers range in color from pink to dark purple.

Swamp sunflower, aka sneezeweed
Helenium
Blooms summer through autumn

FOLIAGE

Burning bush
Euonymus alatus
Bright red autumn foliage

Chinese pistachio
Pistacia chinensis
Foliage in shades of orange, red, and crimson

Flowering dogwood
Cornus florida
Red to reddish-purple foliage, with glossy red fruit

Forsythia
Forsythia
Purple tinge over green to yellow-green foliage

Japanese barberry
Berberis thunbergii
Bright red to orange foliage

Japanese maple
Acer palmatumn
Autumn foliage in yellow, orange, red, or purple

Kousa dogwood
Cornus kousa
Reddish-purple to scarlet foliage

Maple
Acer
Foliage varies from yellow to vibrant scarlet to burgundy.

Smoke bush
Cotinus coggygria
Foliage in yellow, red, and purple

Staghorn sumac
Rhus typhina
Fiery red foliage

Viburnum
Viburnum
Foliage ranges from bright scarlet to orange-red.

Virginia creeper
Parthenocissus quinquefolia
Intense red foliage in autumn

FRUIT

Beautyberry
Callicarpa
Clusters of small purple berries

Crab apple
Malus
Fruits ranging in size and color from dark red to orange and yellow

Cranberry bush viburnum
Viburnum trilobum
Brilliant red fruits turn blue-black and persist into winter.

Persimmon
Diospyros
Fruits in yellow-orange to dark red-orange

Pomegranate
Punica granatum
Fruits persist from autumn through winter.

Rose hips
Rosa
Hips vary in size, shape, and color, from red and orange to dark purple.

SEED HEAD

Chinese lantern
Physalis alkekengi
Orange lantern-shaped pods dangling on long stems

Love-in-the-mist
Nigella
Round, prickly looking seedpods contain black cumin, a culinary spice.

Ornamental onion
Allium
Large spheres of round seedpods held on thin stems

Pincushion flower
Scabiosa
Spheres of multiple seeds held in papery cups

Poppy
Papaver somniferum
Bulbous head topped by a circle with spoke-like rays radiating from the center

Plant Calendar / *Winter*

In **WINTER**, evergreens take center stage. Spruce, cedar, cypress, and pine can scent the house and add color to winter days. Berries, a source of food for birds, also make lovely arrangements. The hardy hellebores with their array of exquisitely sophisticated colors keep the desolation of winter at bay. The ephemeral beauty of hippeastrum grown indoors in the winter months adds a cheerful note to holiday celebrations.

INDOOR BULBS

Dutch iris
Iris hollandica
Flowers in blue, purple, and white

Hippeastrum
Hippeastrum
Flowers in white, pink, coral, and scarlet red, some with stripes and some a mix of colors

Hyacinth
Hyacinthus orientalis
Flowers in blue, white, or yellow

Paper whites
Narcissi
Small, fragrant white flowers

EVERGREEN
The winter evergreens come in colors that range from yellow-green to blue-green and a variety of textures.

Cedar
Cedrus
Long branches with blue-green to green short needles

Cypress
Cupressus
Soft and feathery foliage

Fir
Abies
Pendulous branches with green needles

Spruce
Picea
Blue-green to green needles

Holly
Ilex
Spiky, glossy, deep green foliage traditionally used in Christmas wreaths

Juniper
Juniperis
Bears small blue-green berries

Japanese cedar
Cryptomeria japonica
Whorls of green needles

Japanese cypress
Chamaecyperis
Chartreuse-green, lacy foliage

Rhododendron
Rhododendron
Whorls of glossy, large leaves

Southern magnolia
Magnolia grandiflora
Glossy, large, green leaves with brown suede underside

Olive
Olea europaea
Bears dark fruit on long branches

BERRIES

English ivy
Hedera helix
Clusters of round drupes in dark blue from October to May

Japanese skimmia
Skimmia Japonica
Clusters of red berries persist through winter

Nandina
Nandina domestica
Bright red berries from autumn into winter

Winterberry holly
Ilex verticillata
Red or orange berries through winter

FLOWERING BRANCHES
All flowering branches with buds can be cut early and forced indoors.

Forsythia
Forsythia
Small, bell-shaped yellow flowers

Plum blossom
Prunus mume
Small pale pink flowers

Witch hazel
Hammamelis x intermedia
Spidery flowers in yellow, red, and orange-red

Pussy willow
Salix caprea
Furry-looking silvery flowers

Flowering quince
Chaenomeles
Delicate flowers in red, coral, and pale pink

OUTDOOR BULBS

Snowdrop
Galanthus nivalis
Blooms all winter

Spring snowflake
Leucojum vernum
Blooms late winter

Crocus
Crocus spp.
Blooms late winter

Winter aconite
Eranthis
Yellow buttercup-like flowers bloom late January or early February

FLOWERS

Andromeda
Pieris japonica
Blooms late winter to early spring

Camellia
Camellia sasanqua
Flowers from late autumn to early winter in mild regions

Clematis
Clematis cirrhosa
Winter-blooming evergreen clematis in mild regions

Cyclamen
Cyclamen
Blooms autumn and winter

Hellebore
Helleborus
Blooms from late winter to early spring

Viburnum 'Dawn'
Viburnum bodnantense
Fragrant pink flowers bloom in winter.

Winter heath
Erica
Small, fragrant pink flowers

FLOWERS

A small selection of garden blooms that make great cut flowers throughout the seasons

STAR MAGNOLIA

ASTER

COLUMBINE

CAMELLIA

REDBUD

COSMOS

PURPLE CONEFLOWER

TICKSEED

MOUNTAIN LAUREL

LACE HYDRANGEA

LILY-OF-THE-VALLEY

ASTILBE

IRIS

YARROW

HELENIUM

CRAB APPLE BLOSSOM

FOLIAGE & FRUIT

A sampling of foliage and frut that will make lovely arrangements on their own or in a mixed bouquet

CRAB APPLE

SMOKE BUSH

HOLLY

HOSTA

CYPRESS

JAPANESE MAPLE

JUNIPER

LAMB'S EAR

ROSE HIPS

PURPLE BASIL

POPPY SEED POD

PAINTED FERN

CORAL BELL

LADY'S MANTLE

COLEUS

BARBERRY

Inspiring & Useful Addresses

INSPIRATION Since time immemorial, people have been inspired to bring the beauty of flowers into the home. The art of floral design therefore begins with the appreciation of plants and flowers in the landscape. If you don't have a garden, explore meadows, woodlands, and other natural habitats to see what's growing each season. Observe the ever-changing seasonal plant life along parkways and roadsides. In the city, visit botanical gardens and parks to see plants in their natural context. Here are just a few public gardens that will surely inspire you.

BROOKLYN BOTANIC GARDEN

With more than six thousand plants of myriad species and origins, the Brooklyn Botanic Garden is a great place to explore the wide variety of flowers and plants. The institution is famous for its annual Sakura Matsuri festival, a celebration of the garden's large collection of flowering cherry trees in bloom.

Brooklyn Botanic Garden
900 Washington Avenue
Brooklyn, NY 11225
www.bbg.org

GIVERNY

Monet was greatly interested in botany, and Giverny was his botanical masterpiece and the subject of his paintings for more than twenty years. A lush and watery landscape, Monet's garden is much like his paintings: flecks and dabs of colors as masses of irises, peonies, roses, water lilies, and wisteria run riot at different times of year.

Fondation Claude Monet
Rue Claude Monet 27620
Giverny, France
Giverny.org/gardens/

GREAT DIXTER

The late garden writer and plantsman Christopher Lloyd's spectacular garden at Great Dixter reflects his love of bold, colorful flowers and exotic plants. New and different flower combinations are worked into the border beds throughout the year as varying color experiments are constantly tested and tried.

Great Dixter
Northiam
Rye
East Sussex TN31 6PH
United Kingdom.
www.greatdixter.co.uk

THE HIGH LINE

The Dutch garden designer Piet Oudolf's planting on New York's High Line takes its inspiration from the wild landscape that developed on the disused elevated railroad during the twenty-five years after the trains stopped running. His design emphasizes the beauty of plants through their entire life cycle, from birth through full flowering to dormancy. Designed as a four-season garden, the High Line is the perfect place to experience not only beautiful blooms in spring and summer, but also the exquisite architecture and textures of plants in autumn and winter.

The High Line
210 10th Avenue
New York, NY 1011
www.thehighline.org

NINFA

Known as the most romantic garden in the world, the Garden of Ninfa lies amid a medieval ruin southeast of Rome. With flowering cherries and magnolias exploding in spring, rare climbing roses dripping from ancient walls in summer, and camellias bursting in autumn, the garden changes with every season, offering a tapestry of different colors and scents every month.

Giardino e Rovine de Ninfa
04010 Doganella di Ninfa
Lazio, Italy
www.fondazionecaetani.org

FLOWERS In addition to traditional florists, there are many alternative outlets for flowers. Fresh, seasonal blooms and branches are sold all year round in farmers' markets around the country. In addition, large supermarkets such as Whole Foods have begun offering seasonal flowers that are locally grown. There are also flower farms, some of which specialize in specialty cut flowers. For a listing of flower farms near you, consult the Association of Specialty Cut Flower Growers' website (www.ascfg.org). Another great source of flowers is through the network of Community Supported Agriculture (CSA). The Local Harvest's website (www.localharvest.org) has a listing of CSAs that offer flowers.

FLORAL SUPPLIES

afloral.com
www.afloral.com

B & J Florist Supply Co.
103 West 28th Street
New York, NY 10001
212 564 6086

Jamali Garden
149 West 28th Street
New York, NY 10001
212 244 4025
www.jamaligarden.com

VASES & ACCESSORIES

Astier de Villate
173, rue Saint-Honoré
75001 Paris
(33) 1 42 60 74 13
*Handmade ceramics done
with extremely durable
black terra cotta clay with
a milky white glaze*

Bloom
43 Madison Street
Sag Harbor, NY 11963
631 725 5940
*Impeccably tasteful
antique and new home
accessories and furnishings*

Brook Farm General Store
76 South 6th Street
Brooklyn, NY 11249
718 388 8642
www.brookfarm
generalstore.com
*A wide range of classic,
well-made home
accessories, including
vintage finds*

Canvas Home Store
199 Lafayette Street
New York, NY 10012
212 461 1496
shop.canvashomestore.com
*A great collection of
ceramics, textiles, and glass
accessories for the home*

Erica Tanov
1827 Fourth Street
Berkeley, CA 94710
510 849 3331
www.ericatanov.com
*A small but finely curated
selection of home textiles
and accessories*

Global Table
107-109 Sullivan Street
New York, NY 10012
212 431 5839
www.globaltable.com
*A carefully edited selection
of tabletop and home
accessories from around
the world*

Grdn
103 Hoyt Street
Brooklyn, NY 11217
718 797 3628
Grdnbklyn.com
*Flowers and accessories
for the urban garden*

John Derian
6 East Second Street
New York, NY 10003
212 677 3917
www.johnderian.com
*Beautiful decoupage, hard-
to-find ephemera, and other
fine home accessories*

Layla
86 Hoyt Street
Brooklyn, NY 11201
www.layla-brklyn.com
718 222 1933
*Gorgeous textiles
and accessories from
around the world*

Le Petit Atelier De Paris
31 rue de Montmorency
75003 Paris
(33) 1 44 54 91 40
www.lepetitatelierdeparis.
com
Unique objects for the home

Merci
111 boulevard Beaumarchais
75003 Paris
www.merci-merci.com
*A design-conscious
charity store that offers
flowers, home accessories,
and furnishings*

Ochre
462 Broome Street
New York, NY 10013
212 414 3442
www.ochre.net
*Sophisticated,
contemporary home
accessories and ceramics*

Tail of the Yak
2632 Ashby Avenue
Berkeley, CA 94705
510 841 9891
*A magical treasure
trove of whimsical objects*

Ted Muehling
52 Walker Street
New York, NY 10013
212 431 3825
www.tedmuehling.com
*Exquisitely designed
jewelry and decorative
objects in silver, bronze,
porcelain, and glass*

Terrain
914 Baltimore Pike
Glen Mills, PA 19342
www.shopterrain.com
*A nursery with flowers,
vases, home accessories,
and furnishings*

FLEA MARKETS

Alameda Flea
alamedapointantiquesfaire.
com
*The largest antiques market
in Northern California*

Brooklyn Flea
www.brooklynflea.com
*Everything from flowers
to antiques and crafts*

Le Marché aux Puces de
Vanves
Avenue Marc Sangnier and
Avenue Georges Lafenestre
75014 Paris
Pucesdevanves.typepad.
com
*A smaller and more eclectic
market than the well-known
Clignancourt flea market*

Brimfield Antiques
and Flea Market Show
www.brimfield.com
*The largest outdoor antique
show in the United States*

Acknowledgments

NGOC MINH NGO: I could not have done this book without the help and contribution of many people, to whom I owe my warmest thanks.

To Deborah Needleman, who was the first to listen to my idea of the book and lent her unstinting support by opening the doors to her beautiful homes and letting me cut freely from her garden. To top it all off, she wrote a wonderful foreword.

To Nicolette Owen, who took on this project on blind faith and helped turn my idea into something far more beautiful than I could have imagined. Nicolette's amazing arrangements, passion for all things floral, and willingness to go the extra mile made her a dream collaborator.

To Amy Wilson, who always managed to find the perfect vase and objects for every scenario. Her critical eye, creative support, and loveliness as a person were crucial to the shooting process and made the time we spent together on this project so enjoyable.

To Alayne Patrick, who not only allowed me to take pictures in her beautiful home anytime I wanted, but also lent me amazing objects for my shoots elsewhere. I am eternally grateful for her friendship and constantly inspired by the beauty she creates around her.

To Erica Tanov, Steven Emerson, and Hugo Emerson Tanov, whose generous spirit made my shoot in their lovely home a memorably wonderful experience. I feel extraordinarily blessed to have spent the last day of shooting in their wondrous haven among the trees. The celebratory drink at the end of the day brought the whole project to a lovely finale.

To Scot Schy, who is everything anyone can ask for in a friend and book designer. His thoughtful and elegant design, along with Angela Taormina's expert typography, made this a book that I can be proud of, and I will miss the long hours we labored together in his awesome office.

To Vanessa Holden, who generously gave me time and invaluable feedback whenever I needed it. Her discerning taste and thoughtful opinion helped me to keep everything in check. I am deeply appreciative of her enthusiasm for life and great sense of humor.

To everyone else who allowed me free rein in their lovely homes: Alison Attenborough, Vanessa Holden and Simon Andrews, John Keenen, Keith and Alina McNally, Tamar Mogendorff, Carla and Fernando Music, Deborah Needleman and Jacob Weisberg, Nicolette Owen, Ben Plimpton and Fay Andrada, and Amy Wilson. Each and every one of these places is as unique and inspiring as the people who inhabit them.

To Harriet Maxwell Macdonald and Andrew Corrie, who readily lent me beautiful objects from their lovely store Ochre. To Melissa Goldstein, who continually gave me the encouragement I needed and lent me the perfect blue pitcher for an arrangement. To Sarah Owens, who taught me so much about roses and cut some of the most beautiful flowers for me to photograph.

To Susan Lyall, Tom Sansone, and Austin Sansone, who introduced me to the beautiful meadows of northwest Connecticut. To my sister-in-law, Michele Blackwell, who took me to her favorite haunt to cut blackberry vines. To my brother-in-law, Scott Crider, who has always shared his love of Shakespeare and the classics and encouraged my writing.

To the team at Rizzoli: Dung Ngo, who saw the potential in this book and bravely took it on; Alexandra Tart, who shepherded the project through its long process; and Charles Miers, who allowed me to do the book as I envisioned it.

To my husband, Julian Wass, and my daughter, Lily Wass, whose infinite patience, support, and love help me never to lose sight of the big picture.

NICOLETTE OWEN: To Irene Owen, my mother, for instilling in me a love of flowers and beauty. Your encouragement and love is immeasurable. To Sarah Ryhanen, my dear friend and cohort in all things floral. To Peter St.Lawrence, for your support and friendship, even though I lost your loppers. To Max Gill, for generously letting me into your beautiful cutting garden with a pair of clippers. And finally, to Ngoc and Amy, it's been such a pleasure and privilege to collaborate with you and share our love of flowers and photography. To Deborah Needleman, for always believing in my work.

NGOC MINH NGO is a self-taught
photographer who studied
landscape design at Columbia
University. She has written and
photographed for such magazines
as *Elle Decoration UK*, *Archi-
tectural Digest*, *Martha Stewart
Living*, and *Garden Design*.

NICOLETTE OWEN is the owner
of Nicolette Camille Floral
Design and co-founder of the
Little Flower School in Brooklyn.

DEBORAH NEEDLEMAN was the
founding editor of *Domino*
magazine and is currently the
editor-in-chief of *WSJ Magazine*

FIRST PUBLISHED
in the United States of America in 2012 by
Rizzoli International Publications, Inc.
300 Park Avenue South, New York, NY 10010
www.rizzoliusa.com

© 2012 by Ngoc Minh Ngo
Foreword © 2012 by Deborah Needleman
Book Design by Scot Schy

HAND-PAINTED WALLPAPER
on cover image and endpapers by de Gournay

2012 2013 2014 2015 / 10 9 8 7 6 5 4 3

DISTRIBUTED
in the U.S. trade by Random House, New York

PRINTED IN CHINA

ISBN-13: 978-0-8478-3800-4

Library of Congress Control Number: 2011938528